Atlanta

☆ ☆ ☆

LIBRARY OF CONGRESS CATALOGING-IN-PUBLICATION DATA

Loewen, Nancy, 1964-
  Atlanta / by Nancy Loewen.
    p. cm. -- (Great Cities of the United States)
    Includes index.
  Summary: Introduces the history, economy, and notable attractions of the largest city in Georgia.
  ISBN 0-86592-543-7
  1. Atlanta (Ga.)--Description--Guide-books--Juvenile literature. [1. Atlanta (Ga.)--Description--Guides.] I. Title. II. Series.
F294.A83L63 1989
917.58'2310443--dc20   89-34195
                                                                          CIP
                                                                           AC

☆ ☆ ☆

Atlanta

★ GREAT ★ CITIES ★ OF THE ★ USA ★

TEXT BY
NANCY LOEWEN

DESIGN & PRODUCTION BY
MARK E. AHLSTROM
(The Bookworks)

**ROURKE
ENTERPRISES,
INC.**
Vero Beach, FL 32964
U.S.A.

Symbol of
the New South...

☆ ☆ ☆

TABLE OF CONTENTS

CREDITS

All photos courtesy of the
Atlanta Convention and Visitors Bureau
233 Peachtree Street, NE
Suite 2000, Peachtree Harris Building
Atlanta, Georgia 30303

TYPESETTING AND LAYOUT: THE FINAL WORD
PRINTING: WORZALLA PUBLISHING CO.

☆ ☆ ☆

Symbol of the New South

It's springtime in Atlanta. Steel skyscrapers reflect a bright blue sky. Dogwood and azalea blossoms fill the air with their fresh scents. Kids of all ages play in Atlanta's many parks. Downtown, the streets are crowded with successful business people.

This is Atlanta at its best: Energy and determination mixed with soft Southern beauty. More than any other city, Atlanta is a symbol of the New South. And Atlantans wouldn't have it any other way.

Atlanta, the capital of Georgia, is known for many things. Civil rights leader Martin Luther King, Jr., was born and buried here. Coca-Cola, the drink that changed the taste of America, was invented here in 1886. And two of the world's most popular fictional characters—Scarlet O'Hara and Rhett Butler—had many a quarrel here in Margaret Mitchell's *Gone With The Wind*.

These days, however, Atlanta is recognized less for its past than for its very promising future. As a center of business, Atlanta is thriving. And, with a population that is two-thirds black, Atlanta suffers little of the racial tension seen in other large cities. The city is proud of its record. It provides a good example of what whites and blacks can accomplish when they work together.

A writer for *U.S. News and World Report* called Atlanta "a model for urban racial harmony, power sharing and minority opportunity." Franklin Garrett, director of the Atlanta Historical Society, put it in simpler terms. Atlanta, he once said to *National Geographic*, has always been "forging ahead, gung ho for progress."

With that kind of history, Atlanta is definitely a city to keep an eye on!

In the springtime, dogwood blossoms are a common sight in Atlanta.

ATLANTA THEN & NOW

From Terminus to Atlanta

The Creek Indians lived in the Atlanta area long before white people settled there. By the 1800's, however, white settlers were starting to crowd the Indians out. In 1821, the Creeks were pressured into selling the area of present-day Atlanta to the state of Georgia. And by 1827, the Creeks had sold all their Georgia land. The displaced Indians then moved west, to the Arkansas Territory.

Like many other cities, Atlanta got its start as a railroad town. The state of Georgia began building the Western and Atlantic Railroad in 1836. To mark the southernmost spot of the intended line, an Army engineer put a stake into the ground. It was called the Zero Mile Post.

The next year, a town called Terminus—meaning "to end"—sprang up in that area. Thanks to the railroad, Terminus quickly became a center of trade and transportation.

Today a small monument marks the original site of Terminus. It sits near City Hall in busy downtown Atlanta. No doubt the founders of that long-ago town would be pleased if they could see how their town has grown. Their adventuresome spirit has stayed with the city, through the good times and the bad.

Before Terminus was called Atlanta, it went through one other name change. Governor Lumpkin had worked very hard to bring the railroad to Georgia. The people of Terminus wanted to express their appreciation to him. What better way, they thought, than to name their town after Governor Lumpkin's beloved daughter, Martha? In 1843, Terminus became Marthasville.

The railroad center kept the name Marthasville until 1845. At that time, railroad engineer J. Edgar Thompson renamed the town Atlanta, after the Atlantic Railroad. Two years later, Atlanta was incorporated as a city.

"The destiny of Atlanta was pegged from the start to be a transportation and distribution center, and that's what it still is," commented "Mr. Atlanta," Franklin Garrett. "By 1860, four railroad lines met in the city. It was a noisy place, picturesque, but noisy."

Battle Calls

By the start of the Civil War in 1861, Atlanta's population had grown to 10,000. Most of its citizens supported their state when Georgia seceded, or withdrew, from the Union on January 19, 1861.

Like most Southern states, Georgia's economy was based on cotton—and on keeping black slaves to grow that cotton. Most people in the North, however, thought slavery was wrong. When the Illinois politician named Abraham Lincoln was elected President of the United States in 1860, Southerners were worried that slavery would be abolished.

The Southern states wanted the freedom to make their own decision on slavery and other issues. They formed what was to be their own nation, the Confederate States of America. But to the Union, such a division was unthinkable. Compromise seemed out of the question. The Civil War began when Confederate troops opened fire on Fort Sumter, South Carolina, on April 12, 1861.

Atlanta was very important in the Confederate war effort. As an arsenal, the city both made and stored the guns and other military equipment needed for the war. Factories—making everything from buttons to saddles and guns—were built at a record pace. Atlanta's citizens did all they could to help "their boys" win the war. Even the churches donated their iron bells to be turned into cannon barrels!

But Atlanta's importance to the South also put the city in great danger. During the spring and summer of 1864, General William T. Sher-

Grant Park, named for Lemuel P. Grant, is Atlanta's oldest park. It is home to the Atlanta Zoo and the Cyclorama.

man and his Union troops mounted a campaign to overtake Atlanta. The Confederate troops, under the direction of General Joseph Johnston and, later, General John Hood, were given the job of defending Atlanta.

At first, few Atlantans admitted that they were worried. "Atlanta will never fall!" they boasted. "Our boys will send those Yanks whimpering back to the north!" But the Union troops just moved closer and closer to the city.

Atlanta now received a firsthand glimpse of the tragedy of war. Train-loads of wounded soldiers were brought into the city. Volunteer nurses helped care for these men in Atlanta hospitals. As difficult as that was, however, it was only a hint of what was to come.

On July 20, near gentle Peachtree Creek, the blue and the gray forces clashed in battle. Fighting with all their strength, the Confederates managed to beat the Yankees back to the banks of the creek. But, outnumbered as they were, the Confederate soldiers couldn't hold their advantage. The Union troops pushed forward.

That day the first Union shell was fired into Atlanta. It killed a little girl.

On July 22, the two sides faced each other again in the Battle of Atlanta. Atlantans huddled in their cellars, covering their ears to block out the sounds of war. Nearly 8,000 Confederate soldiers lost their lives in that battle—more than twice the casualties suffered by the Union troops. When the fighting was over, General Sherman was even closer to the city.

With three of its railroad lines cut off and the fourth controlled by the enemy, Atlanta fell on September 2, 1864. Union troops had established themselves in the heart of the Confederacy.

General Sherman understood how important Atlanta was to the South. He knew there must be no question of Atlanta's defeat. He ordered Atlanta evacuated, then had his troops set fire to the city. By the time the Union forces left, Atlanta lay in ashes. Of the 3,600 buildings in Atlanta, only 400 were left standing.

Though he had caused its destruction, General Sherman knew that the city of Atlanta would rise again. "The same reason which caused me to destroy Atlanta will make it a great city in the future," Sherman once said to a young Atlanta reporter. He was right.

Beginning Again

America's bloodiest war came to an end on April 9, 1865. Though the damage was extensive, the Civil War did help bring about some positive changes in the South. The most important one, of course, was that slavery was ended. Adjusting to this new situation was not easy. The bitterness of both the black and white people has lasted for generations.

Another change was a new kind of Southern industrialism. Until the

The Cyclorama is a painting 50 feet high and 400 feet in circumference. With three-dimensional figures, sound, light effects, and narration, the Cyclorama depicts the Battle of Atlanta in 1864.

Civil War, rich people put all their money into land and slaves, rather than things like factories, mines, and mills. The South had to depend on the North for products such as glass, furniture, paper, and farm machinery. But the war forced the South to produce these things for itself. Wartime factories were converted into peacetime factories in order to make products Southerners could both use and sell.

Defeated in war but not in spirit, Atlanta set about rebuilding itself. New buildings were constructed. Businesses were established. People came to the transformed city by the thousands, and Atlanta was once more a leading city of the South.

In 1866 Atlanta was named the federal headquarters for Reconstruction in the surrounding area. And on April 20, 1868, the city replaced Milledgeville as the capital of the state of Georgia.

Atlanta honors its past in its choice of a municipal emblem: a phoenix rising out of flames. In an ancient Egyptian myth, a phoenix was a lovely bird that lived in the desert. Every 500 years, the phoenix would consume itself by fire. But from the ashes rose a new bird, ready to live for another period.

Good Times & Bad

By 1900, Atlanta had a population of more than 90,000. What had started out as a railroad settlement among scrub pines had, in little more than 60 years, turned into a thriving manufacturing center.

Contributing to Atlanta's growth were several big fairs, which drew worldwide attention to the city. In 1881, Atlanta hosted the International Cotton Exposition. This was one of the first international fairs ever held in the United States. Afterwards, even more businesses moved to the area.

Still enjoying the taste of success, Atlanta next hosted the Piedmont Exposition in 1887. Its theme was the cooperation between agriculture and industry. Attending the Exposition were none other than President Grover Cleveland and his wife.

A phoenix tops the statue "Atlanta from the Ashes." The phoenix is a mythical bird that died by fire and rose from the ashes, as Atlanta did.

Eight years later, in 1895, Atlanta hosted the Cotton States and International Exposition. This show featured the 10 cotton states and the resources they had to offer. A group of blacks had their own building at this Exposition. Their featured speaker was Booker T. Washington, a famous black educational leader.

Many white Southerners had not yet come to terms with the concept of black equality. At no time was this more evident than in 1906, when Atlanta suffered its worst race riots. The trouble started when Hoke Smith, a man who wanted to keep blacks from voting, was elected governor of Georgia in a landslide election. His campaign and election seemed to magnify the resentment whites and blacks felt toward each other.

About a month after Smith's election, the tension exploded into four days of intense rioting. Ten black people were killed, along with two white people. More than 60 blacks were wounded. Not since the Civil War had Georgia seen such violence.

Forward Atlanta!

Atlanta steadily continued to grow. During World War II, military operations and new industries related to the war came to the city. Many rural people moved to Atlanta to take the newly created defense jobs.

In 1952, Atlanta annexed 81 square miles of surrounding land. This boosted its population by 100,000. By 1960, about 487,000 people were living in Atlanta.

Yet Atlanta wanted more. In 1961, the city set out on a mission: to prove to the world that Atlanta was **the** place to be. Under a program called "Forward Atlanta," the city advertised itself in the leading business magazines, hoping to attract new businesses to the area.

The program worked. Within three years, nearly 600 branches of national companies had been established in the city. Many of the buildings that make up Atlanta's impressive skyline were built in this period.

Atlanta's economic growth has continued into the 1980's. Between

Atlanta's skyline takes on a special beauty at night.

1983 and 1988, businesses invested nearly $52 billion in the city. The Chamber of Commerce sometimes calls Atlanta "The City Without Limits"—and with good reason.

During the 1950's and '60's, Atlanta was also known for its progress on racial issues. In 1957, Martin Luther King, Jr., and others established the Southern Christian Leadership Conference. This organization coordinated the work of civil rights groups, strengthening the movement. Today, Atlanta is still considered a black political power center.

INSIDE ATLANTA

The Throbbing Heart

Atlanta sits on the Piedmont Plateau in northwest Georgia, amid rolling hills and pine trees. With an elevation of nearly 1,050 feet, Atlanta has the third-highest elevation of major U.S. cities. The Blue Ridge Mountains rise to the northwest of the city. Nearby, the Chattahoochee River makes its way to the southwest, where it forms part of the border between Georgia and Alabama.

Atlanta is a sprawling city. The "city proper" covers more than 132 square miles, mostly in Fulton County. Atlanta's suburbs, however, are located in 18 counties—over a territory of nearly 5,200 square miles! More than 2.6 million people live in the Atlanta metro area.

The oldest and most famous street in Atlanta is Peachtree Street. It started out as a winding trail along the Chattahoochee River, between Terminus and an Indian trading post called Standing Peachtree. Today it runs from the central business district to the northern residential area.

One of the most impressive projects in the downtown area is a modern business complex called Peachtree Center. It has just about anything a person could want—hotels, office buildings, restaurants, and convention and entertainment facilities. Westin Peachtree Plaza, 73 mirrored stories high, is one of the tallest hotels in America. Peachtree Center also includes the two largest wholesale markets in the Southeast, the Merchandise Mart and the Apparel Mart.

Everything in Peachtree Center is within easy walking distance of everything else. As people walk from one point to another, they can

The Georgia State Capitol Building in downtown Atlanta was built in 1889 with a dome of gold leaf that was mined from the North Georgia mountains.

enjoy the contemporary sculpture that sits in open garden plazas. Or they can do some people-watching from the glass-enclosed skywalks.

Peachtree Center was designed by world-renowned architect John Portman. He once described the Center as a "village in the center of the whole throbbing heart of a great city." It's no wonder that Peachtree Center is sometimes called the Rockefeller Center of the South.

Southeast of Peachtree Center is the Atlanta City Hall, the State Capitol, and other government buildings. Atlantans are especially proud of their capitol building, which is patterned after the national capitol in Washington, D. C. There is one big difference, however. The dome on Georgia's capitol is covered with gold leaf, mined within the state. It's especially pretty on sunny days!

Five Points is a famous intersec-

Robert W. Woodruff Memorial Park is just north of "Five Points," the center of Atlanta. The area was donated by Coca-Cola businessman Robert W. Woodruff.

tion in downtown Atlanta. Clustered around it are many beautiful banks, stores, and office buildings. Three miles away, in Inman Park, Little Five Points is a more casual version of the same.

Other important structures include the huge World Congress Center and the Omni International Complex. Both of these have contributed a great deal toward Atlanta's reputation as a convention city. Another attraction is the CNN Center, which houses the broadcast studios for Cable News Network (CNN).

Contrasts

The sense of wealth and well-being found in downtown Atlanta is also found in some residential areas. Atlanta's northern suburbs form an area known as the Golden Crescent. Many of the people who live there are very rich.

In the northern suburb of Buckhead, for example, many residents don't just live in houses. They live in mansions! This is where the governor's mansion is located, along with the homes of other famous Atlantans.

The shopping centers in Buckhead are among most expensive in the world. Names such as Neiman Marcus, Gucci, Laura Ashley, and others are common. There are also many fashionable boutiques and trendy restaurants.

Not all of Atlanta is wealthy, however. In fact, poverty and homelessness are two of Atlanta's biggest problems.

Within Atlanta's southern suburbs are many poor neighborhoods. These form a startling contrast with the splendor of northern Atlanta. On the south side of the city, for instance, is an area called Zone 3. Nearly one-third of Atlanta's public housing projects are located here. Many of the houses in this neighborhood are little more than shacks. It's not unusual to see outhouses in the small back yards.

Unemployment, drug abuse, and crime are widespread in Zone 3, which police refer to as the "combat zone." Many people there are bat-

The Georgia Governor's mansion was built in 1968 in the Greek Revival style of architecture. It houses a collection of antiques, and is open for public tours.

tling an addiction to crack, a highly dangerous form of cocaine. Other people make and sell their own corn liquor. But this, too, is illegal and dangerous. If it's not made correctly or if people consume too much, corn liquor can—and does—kill.

Cabbagetown is another poor neighborhood. As one of the few "ethnic" areas in Atlanta, it has a history very different from that of Zone 3. Cabbagetown was settled by people from the Appalachian mountains, who came to work in the Fulton Bag & Cotton Mill. Then the mill closed in 1980, taking away a major source of jobs. Many of the families chose to stay in the neighborhood, however. Their Appalachian heritage is still important to them.

Educating Atlanta

As Atlanta's business interests continue to expand, a trend has developed which many people find disturbing. More and more offices are being built in the northern suburbs, instead of in the city itself. Middle-class white people are leaving the central city in large numbers in order to live closer to the jobs. This is known as "white flight." Many other large cities are facing this problem as well.

One of the effects of white flight is on the public schools. Though Atlanta peacefully integrated its schools in the 1960's, the shifting white population has left Atlanta's public school system 90 percent black. Today, Atlanta's schools—about 115 public elementary and high schools—are among the most racially segregated in the nation.

Atlanta is home to about 20 four-year colleges, universities, and other schools. The city's largest university is Georgia State University. Emory University and the Georgia Institute of Technology are important research institutes. Atlanta also has the largest complex of black schools in the U.S., the Atlanta University Center. Martin Luther King, Jr., graduated from the Center's Morehouse College.

☆☆☆

Higher Education in Atlanta

Art Institute of Atlanta
Atlanta Area Technical School
Atlanta Christian College
Atlanta College of Art
Atlanta College of Medical and Dental Careers
Atlanta Junior College
Atlanta University
Bauder Fashion College
Clark College
Emory University
Georgia Institute of Technology
Georgia State University
Gupton-Jones College of Funeral Services
Interdenominational Theological Center
Mercer University
Mercer University Southern School of Pharmacy
Morehouse College
Morehouse School of Medicine
Morris Brown College
National Center for Paralegal Training
Oglethorpe University
Southern Technical Institute
Spelman College

GETTING AROUND

In 1855, Atlanta became the first city to use gas streetlights. And by 1890, the city had the most complete system of street railways in the nation. A century later, Atlantans hold another transportation record. On average, Atlantans spend more on their cars than do people in any other U.S. city!

Even with high-speed expressways, heavy traffic always seems to be a problem. The downtown area is congested during rush hours. Driving to the suburbs after work can be a tiring, bumper-to-bumper experience. In the short term, this problem is made worse by construction projects to widen the expressways. Hopefully, however, these improvements will soon bring a little relief to commuters.

While rush-hour traffic may be stressful, at least Atlanta doesn't face the parking shortage so many other large cities must deal with. Though little on-street parking is available downtown, there are plenty of parking garages and lots. Many of these charge as little as $2 a day, although rates are quite a bit higher near places such as the CNN Center and the World Congress Center.

Atlanta also has a unique and highly praised system of mass transportation, called MARTA. That stands for Metropolitan Atlanta Rapid Transit Authority. MARTA is a combination bus and rapid rail system. For just 75 cents, people can ride on MARTA vehicles all day.

There are some serious problems facing MARTA, however. The main one is that the system doesn't yet run in the areas where it's needed most—the poor suburbs, where few people own cars. People living in the southern suburbs have a hard time getting to the better jobs, increasingly found

Atlanta's rapid rail system provides speedy and economical transportation. The rail and bus system is called MARTA—Metropolitan Atlanta Rapid Transit Authority.

in the north. They often end up taking low-paying temporary jobs closer to their homes. Others do manage to commute, but at a heavy price. It can take as long as four hours—one way—to get from the southern suburbs to the northern ones!

Some people blame racism and class discrimination for this problem. The richer counties, they say, don't want to improve their mass transit system because they don't want poor people moving in. Still, many Atlantans are trying hard to extend the benefits of MARTA to more of Atlanta's citizens.

THE MAIN ATTRACTIONS

People Who Made a Difference

Martin Luther King, Jr., was born on Atlanta's Auburn Avenue in 1929. His father was the pastor of the Ebenezer Baptist Church, also on Auburn Avenue. King, too, eventually pastored that little church—and much of the world as well. With a commitment to nonviolence and a gift for public speaking, King became the main leader of the civil rights movement in the 1950's and '60's.

In 1964, King won the Nobel

Martin Luther King, Jr., an Atlanta native, is buried here on Auburn Avenue, a block from the house in which he was born and near the Baptist Church where he preached.

Peace Prize for his work. Four years later, on April 4, 1968, the great leader was assassinated while showing support for a sanitation workers' strike in Memphis.

Atlanta and its visitors pay tribute to King at the Martin Luther King, Jr., National Historic Site. One of Atlanta's most visited places, it stretches along a two-block area on Auburn Avenue. The site includes King's birthplace, tomb, and church.

The Carter Presidential Center stands on a hill overlooking downtown Atlanta. Jimmy Carter was governor of Georgia from 1971 to 1975. The next year, the native of Plains, Georgia, was elected the 39th President of the United States.

Inside the Carter Presidential Center is the Jimmy Carter Library. Stored here are more than 27 million documents and photographs from Carter's administration! Also operating out of the Center are the Carter Center of Emory University, a research institute, and the Carter-Menil Human Rights Foundation.

Ted Turner is another person whose influence is felt in Atlanta— and in the world. In 1970, Turner purchased an Atlanta television station. Six years later, he had transformed it into SuperStation WTBS, the first television station to use satellite technology. Today the Superstation reaches 38 million homes over 7,000 cable systems.

In 1980, Ted Turner changed the television industry once again with the introduction of a 24-hour news station called Cable News Network. CNN has since won many journalism awards. Following that success, Turner established the Headline News Network. This network offers 30-minute newscasts around the clock. Incidentally, Ted Turner is also the owner of the Atlanta Hawks basketball team.

The Arts

Atlanta is a city that supports the arts. Visitors and residents alike will always find plenty going on, from art exhibits to plays, concerts, and readings.

The Robert W. Woodruff Arts Center is found on Peachtree Street.

At night, the Atlanta High Museum of Art looks like a work of art itself.

It houses the Atlanta Children's Theater, the Alliance Theater, the Atlanta Opera, the Atlanta College of Art, and more. The complex is operated by the Atlanta Arts Alliance.

Also in the Woodruff Arts Center is the Atlanta Symphony Orchestra. From 1967 to 1988, the orchestra was directed by Robert Shaw—perhaps the best choral conductor in the world. Though he has stepped down from his position at the orchestra,

Shaw is still important to the city of Atlanta. He is now heading the Robert Shaw Institute at Emory University.

Near the Robert W. Woodruff Arts Center is the High Museum of Art. Covered with white porcelain panels, the six-level building is very modern-looking. Skylights and big windows dispel any thoughts of a "stuffy museum." The High Museum of Art is famous for Renaissance paintings, but it has many other permanent exhibits. There's even a

Sports fans in Atlanta were thrilled when the Atlanta-Fulton County Stadium opened in 1965. The stadium is the home of baseball's Atlanta Braves and football's Atlanta Falcons.

gallery just for children, called Spectacle.

The Atlanta Ballet was founded in 1927, making it the oldest civic ballet company in the country. The dancers give performances in the Civic Center Auditorium and Fox Theater.

Each fall, the Atlanta Arts Festival is held in Piedmont Park. There people stroll through art exhibits, listen to concerts, and attend dance programs. Atlanta went all out for the arts in the summer of 1988, when it hosted the National Black Arts Festival. This inspiring event cost $1.8 million to put on!

Sports & Recreation

1965 marked the completion of the Atlanta-Fulton County Stadium. This was an exciting prospect for Atlanta sports fans. They hoped the new stadium would bring professional sports teams to their city—and their optimism paid off.

Today Atlanta has two professional sports teams playing in the stadium. The Atlanta Braves baseball team plays in the West division of the National League. And the Atlanta Falcons play football in the Western Division of the National Football Conference. Basketball fans can watch the Atlanta Hawks play in the newer Omni Coliseum.

College football is another big hit with Atlantans. Perhaps one team in particular has something to do with that—the Georgia Tech Yellow Jackets. This team's first coach was the legendary John Heisman. Today's Heisman Trophy, given each year to the best U.S. college football player, is named for him.

For people who want to do more than watch sports, the Chattahoochee River provides plenty of entertainment. Atlanta natives fondly refer to the river as "the Hooch." Canoeing, boating, and rafting are popular activities in nice weather—which, in

Rafting on the Chattahoochee River is a popular sport in the Atlanta area. The Chatta-hoochee National Recreation Area is part of the U.S. National Parks system.

Atlanta's mild climate, is much of the time.

Racing fans can find plenty of action at the Atlanta International Raceway, which features NASCAR racing. Other kinds of racing—including Formula One, sports car, and motorcycle—take place at Road Atlanta, near Gainesville.

Parks

Unlike some large cities, Atlanta is not overwhelmed by concrete. More than 5,000 acres of parks and playgrounds are in the Atlanta area.

Grant Park was named after railroad tycoon Colonel Lemuel Grant. Besides being home to the Atlanta Zoo, Grant Park has another special exhibit called the Cyclorama. This is a circular painting of 1864's Battle of Atlanta. But it's not just an ordinary painting. The Cyclorama stands 42 feet high and 358 feet around! It was finished in 1886 by a group of German artists.

Visiting the Cyclorama can be a dramatic experience. As visitors look at the battle scenes, they hear gun shots and cannon booms. Strains of "Dixie" and "The Battle Hymn of the Republic" can be heard above the groans of wounded men.

Stone Mountain Park is located east of Atlanta. Standing 825 feet above the surrounding plain, Stone Mountain is the largest granite rock in the world. It measures more than five miles around its base! Some scientists think that the unusual mountain is 300 million years old.

Size is not the only thing that makes Stone Mountain unique. Carved into the northern face of the mountain are figures of the South's Civil War heroes. The sculpture—as long as a city block—shows Confederate President Jefferson Davis, General Robert E. Lee, and General Thomas "Stonewall" Jackson. The figure of Lee is as tall as a nine-story building!

This grand-scale sculpture was begun in 1923. Five years later, funds for the project ran out. The unfinished figures of Davis, Lee, and Jackson rested in the side of the mountain for years. Then, in 1964, work on the project began again.

Carved in granite at Stone Mountain Memorial Park are Confederate Generals Robert E. Lee and "Stonewall Jackson" and Confederate President Jefferson Davis.

Stone Mountain Memorial Park, east of Atlanta, has the world's largest granite formation. The park has facilities for sports and entertainment, copies of Civil War locomotives, and a historic Southern plantation.

Under the direction of sculptor Walker Hancock, the massive sculpture was finished in 1969.

Stone Mountain Park has plenty of other things to do as well. On the enormous park grounds are an ice-skating rink, water park, and golf course. In the summer, a laser show called "Night on Stone Mountain" is shown to the park's visitors.

Also near Atlanta is Six Flags Over Georgia, an amusement park. Besides various shows, the park has more than 100 rides. These include the 10-story free-fall ride, the white water rafting adventure and the Z-force steel roller coaster. Obviously these rides are not for the weak of heart—or stomach!

The Great American Scream Machine at Six Flags Over Georgia is one of more than 100 attractions at the 33-acre family entertainment park.

INDUSTRY & TRADE

"Atlanta is building its history now. **This** is its golden age of development," said Atlanta Mayor Andrew Young in 1988. Looking at the facts, it would be hard to argue with that statement.

In 1987 alone, $16 billion in new businesses came into the city. About 450 of the Fortune 500 companies have offices in Atlanta. And with more than 130 banking and investment firms, Atlanta is a major financial center.

Atlanta is among the top three convention cities in the nation. Facilities such as the World Congress Center and the Omni International Complex have contributed to its reputation in that area. To house all the convention-goers, Atlanta offers more than 43,500 hotel rooms!

From July 18-21, 1988, Atlanta was in the national spotlight as host of the 1988 National Democratic Convention. It was the first national political convention in the Deep South since the Civil War. In Atlanta, Massachusetts governor Michael Dukakis received his party's nomination for President of the United States. Here, too, Reverend Jesse Jackson delivered one of his most memorable speeches.

In Atlanta's metropolitan area, manufacturing is big business. Nearly 3,000 companies make such items as cars, chemicals, aircraft, iron and steel products, soft drinks, furniture, and textiles.

Government-related business, too, plays an important part in the city. One name that comes up quite often in the news is the Centers for Disease Control, located near Emory University. The CDC is part of the U.S. Department of Health and Human Services. Scientists at CDC research diseases, track down sources of epidemics, and provide health information to the public.

Atlanta began as a center of transportation, and it has easily managed to hold on to that title. Trains carrying people and freight are always on the move. Atlanta trucking companies transport goods all across the nation.

Though the early railroad workers at Terminus never dreamed of such amazing contraptions as airplanes, flight is a major Atlanta industry as well. Atlanta's Hartsfield International Airport is one of the world's busiest in number of flights. It is also the biggest employment center in the state of Georgia, providing jobs for nearly 36,000 people!

Busy as it is, Hartsfield International still has a touch of Atlanta class. Travelers from all over the world enjoy looking at the collection of contemporary art showcased within the airport.

Of course, no account of Atlanta's industries would be complete without mentioning Atlanta's favorite beverage. Way back in 1886, an Atlantan druggist named "Doc" Pemberton invented a syrup he called Coca-Cola. Mixing the syrup in a three-legged pot in his backyard, Doc sold 25 gallons the first year. He pocketed about $50.

Atlanta likes being the birthplace of one of the world's most famous drinks. At one point, even the local zoo showed its support—naming four of its elephants Coca, Cola, Delicious, and Refreshing!

Today Coca-Cola still has its headquarters in Atlanta. Besides contributing a great deal to the local economy, the company benefits Atlanta in other ways as well. Endowments are given to schools and other organizations. Working with the government, the company also makes an effort to solve city problems.

GOVERNING THE PEOPLE

Atlanta has a mayor-council form of government. Voters elect the mayor, city council president, and 18 members of the city council to four-year terms. Property taxes paid by Atlanta citizens and businesses provide the city government with most of its money.

Politically, Atlanta's progressive nature became clear for all to see in 1969. That year, Atlanta voters elected Sam Massell, Jr., a Jew, as mayor. A black politician named Maynard Jackson was elected as vice mayor. Four years later, in 1973, Maynard Jackson himself was elected mayor. He was the first black to be elected mayor of a major Southern city.

Another prominent black leader, Andrew Young, took over the job of mayor in 1981. Young had worked closely with Martin Luther King, Jr. He had also been the Deep South's first black congressman in 70 years. In 1985, Atlanta voters re-elected Young.

Blacks hold other important city government positions as well. As of 1988, five of seven seats on the Fulton County Commission are filled by blacks. They hold half of Atlanta City Council jobs. And they control 22 of the city's 36 government bureaus.

Atlanta can take pride in its record of black representation, which is perhaps the best of any major U.S. city. However, it's important to remember that Atlanta's population is about two-thirds black. Atlanta has come a long way toward equal representation, but the journey's not over yet.

Atlanta is a progressive city.

FINDING A BETTER WAY

Like any city or town, Atlanta has its share of problems. One of them relates again to the racial issue. Though whites and blacks seem to get along well when it comes to business, there is still little social mixing. Until blacks and whites can come together as friends, a complete understanding between the races will not be possible.

Ironically, the most urgent problem in the prosperous city of Atlanta is poverty. The economic growth Atlanta is experiencing has yet to improve the lives of Atlanta's many poor people. In fact, it's almost like there are two different Atlantas. One consists of modern skyscrapers and high-stakes business deals. The other consists of crowded housing projects and an attitude of despair.

About 27 percent of Atlanta's population falls below the federal poverty level. Only Newark, New Jersey, has a bigger percentage of poor people. And the difference between the rich and the poor seems to be growing worse. Many people are very concerned about this situation.

More than 48,000 Atlantans live in public housing projects. Another 6,000 are homeless—with the numbers growing larger every year. By 1988, Atlanta had built 52 shelters for the homeless. While such shelters are needed, they're far from being the answer.

Community groups are putting pressure on the government to build more low-rent apartments, and to provide more direct-aid programs such as job training. The expansion of the mass transit system, MARTA, would be another step forward.

Some Atlantans have taken matters into their own hands. In 1987, a bunch of young architects and their friends formed a group called the "Mad Housers." Whenever they get the chance, they put up small huts for homeless people in need of shelter. The group's motto: "We build huts because we're nuts!"

The Mad Housers build their huts on unused private and public land, usually in wooded areas. They don't bother to get building permits or other necessary permission. Because of this, the city government can't really approve of what they're doing. Still, the Mad Housers haven't been challenged very often. "Our huts are a symbol of immediate action," said one Mad Houser to *People Weekly* in 1988.

Other, more formal groups are also trying to ease the tension in Atlanta. The Southern Regional Council, a policy research group, is one example. Action Forum is another. It was formed by black and white business executives, who are working together to solve community problems. There's also the Community Relations Commission, formed to help people find jobs and to improve relations between the races. It has 22 members, appointed by the mayor.

Along Auburn Avenue, Coretta Scott King continues the work of her late husband at the Martin Luther King, Jr., Center for Social Change. The organization works with issues such as prison reform and voter registration.

Though no city will ever be problem-free, Atlanta is trying to make its opportunities available to more of its citizens. "I think Atlanta is the kind of town where one person can still make a difference," says Owen Montague of the Atlanta Exchange, an organization of black professionals.

Atlanta, it seems clear, will not let up in its fight for progress.

Atlantans enjoy a pleasant day at a park near Five Points.

*Atlanta, Georgia

IMPORTANT FACTS

- Population: 421,910 (1986 estimate)
  Rank: 32
- Population of metropolitan area: 2,560,500
  Rank: 13
- Mayor: Andrew Young (next election
  January 1990)
- Fulton and DeKalb Counties
- Capital of Georgia

- Land area: 136 sq. miles
- Monthly normal temperature:
  January—41.9°F
  July—78.6°F
- Average annual precipitation: 48.61"
- Latitude: 33° 45' 10" N
- Longitude: 84° 23' 37" W
- Altitude: ranges from 940 ft. to 1,050 ft.

- Time zone: Eastern

- Annual events:
  Atlanta Dogwood Festival, April
  Georgia Renaissance Festival, April-June
  Atlanta Golf Classic, June
  Atlanta Hunt and Steeplechase, April

IMPORTANT DATES

1821—Creek Indians sold land of present-
day Atlanta to the state of Georgia.
1837—A town called Terminus sprang up at
southern end of Western & Atlantic
Railroad.
1843—Terminus renamed Marthasville.
1845—Marthasville renamed Atlanta.
1847—Atlanta incorporated as a city.
1861-1865—Civil War.
1864—Atlanta fell to General Sherman and
the Union troops.
1868—Atlanta became capital of Georgia.
1880's & '90's—Atlanta hosted several well-
attended expositions.
1906—race riots.
1952—Atlanta annexed 81 square miles of
surrounding land.
1960's—A program called "Forward Atlanta"
attracted new businesses to area.
1964—Martin Luther King, Jr., won Nobel
Peace Prize.
1973—Maynard Jackson elected mayor, first
black mayor of major Southern city.
1988—National Democratic Convention held
in Atlanta.

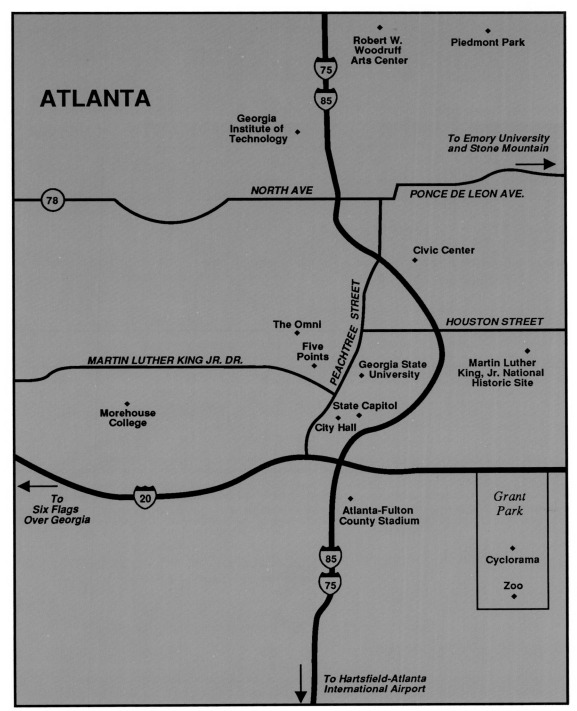

ATLANTA

Robert W. Woodruff Arts Center

Piedmont Park

Georgia Institute of Technology

To Emory University and Stone Mountain

NORTH AVE

PONCE DE LEON AVE.

78

Civic Center

PEACHTREE STREET

HOUSTON STREET

The Omni

Five Points

MARTIN LUTHER KING JR. DR.

Georgia State University

Martin Luther King, Jr. National Historic Site

State Capitol

City Hall

Morehouse College

To Six Flags Over Georgia

20

Atlanta-Fulton County Stadium

Grant Park

85

75

Cyclorama

Zoo

To Hartsfield-Atlanta International Airport

©1989 Mark E. Ahlstrom

★ GLOSSARY ★

architect—a person who designs buildings and overlooks their construction.

assassinated—to be killed by a sudden or secret attack, usually for political reasons.

civil rights—the rights of citizens guaranteed by the United States Constitution and by acts of Congress. This phrase usually refers to the struggle of blacks and other minorities to be treated fairly under the law.

commute—to travel a fairly long distance to work every day, whether by car or mass transportation. A person who commutes is called a commuter.

contemporary—modern; current.

convention—a large assembly of people meeting for a common purpose, usually over a period of several days.

Deep South—The region in the United States that consists of Alabama, Georgia, Louisiana, Mississippi, and South Carolina.

elevation—the height of land above sea level.

exposition—a large public display or show. Similar to a convention.

gold leaf—a very thin layer of gold.

incorporated—the legal establishment of a city.

mass transit—public transportation such as buses and subways.

metropolis—a large important city and its suburbs.

municipal—having to do with city government.

New South—A term referring to the South in the period since the 1960's, marked by a growing economy and racial integration.

Palladian—a style of architecture that is similar in some ways to ancient Greek and Roman architecture.

plateau—a large area of land that is higher than the land that surrounds it.

porcelain—a very hard, thin material often used to make dishes and plates.

Reconstruction—the reorganization of the Southern states in the period after the Civil War.

representation—in government, having an elected official who will speak for one's concerns.

secede—to officially withdraw from an organization.

tycoon—a business leader with a great deal of power and wealth.

INDEX